Your Regular Non-linear 35 Year Old

Life stories and observations near midlife crisis

Piyali Kar

Made with ❤ on the BookLeaf Publishing Platform
www.bookleafpub.in
www.bookleafpub.com

Dedication

To my pillars of Kindness and Strength
Mimmi and Baba,
Thank You for being you.

Preface

At every stage of my life, I have dared to question myself. I believe it takes nothing more, and nothing less, to live a non-linear life. The willingness to rub against your own edges, until your true self slowly reveals itself. It is through these small, persistent enquiries that certain dilemmas of life have appeared before me — clear, and sometimes painfully honest. In each of these truths, I have found myself guided by curiosity, by wilderness and the oddities of nature itself.

These poems were written over six years, from 2019 to 2025 — years that shaped and reshaped me, each one distinct, each one leaving me more tender, raw and human. And always, it was nature who held my hand and gently divided these experiences for me, like seasons unfolding their quiet, predictable magic.

I grew to love the slow, unhurried life of mountain villages during these years. That life, simple, bare, and generous, became my greatest teacher, introducing me to the cyclic nature of existence. Much like the Earth's quiet revolutions around the sun, our lives too are carved into four humble seasons:

Autumn — for shedding. For letting go of what we once held dear, but which no longer serves us.
Winter — for resting. For resting and observing life's quiet lessons and gathering strength for the unseen blooms ahead.
Spring — for learning. For tending to the fragile self and nurturing it, so it may someday stand tall and rooted like an old tree.
Summer — for playing. Life, after all, is one great playground, and we are meant to enjoy it, to live uninhibitedly and honestly, like children.

Each poem in this book was born from a lesson, a moment of observation, where I stood not as the hero of the story, but as its narrator. My words are deeply subjective, but I hope, as you read them, you will find small echoes between your life and mine and everything in between that connects all of us. I am, at best, an imperfect observer of the billions of impressions life leaves on us each day. But what remains sacred to me is this: Love, Growth, and Compassion for all living things, fierce, unbiased, and endless.
I am someone who tries to find a little bit of magic in the

everyday, gathering these tiny fragments into one large, comforting bowl of happy soup I hope to drink at the end of this life.

The Autumn collection holds the earliest poems — reflections on a time when I began deviating from what I call 'linear living.' It was a time of seeking: love, meaning, and words. In 2019, I quit my job. I believed the life I was leading, and the identity I had built, were slowly making me lose both love and my passion for writing. I wanted to shed my skin and walk a path that would lead me closer to my "North" — a direction marked by a nurturing, loving environment and a quiet devotion to writing. In Therapy and I, I recall my early struggles — and the brave, deliberate choice to seek help, to untangle the chaos inside my mind. That act of self-love saved me. Pancake and Love was written after my first breakup at 29. A quiet rebellion against the dating culture and my own tangled understanding of love. Threshold of A Midlife Crisis emerged during this time too, as I sought refuge in theatre and meditation to fill the hollow spaces growing within me. Non-linear Living is the poem that taught me how nature, in its smallest, most overlooked parts, teaches us freedom. Each leaf, different from the next, growing in whatever shape gives it the best chance at life. Choosing my own path never felt more right than on a solo trip to Manali, in 2019. There, among strangers who paused to look at the world differently, I dared to call myself a writer.

The Winter collection is woven from my first year in Himachal Pradesh. Six months after leaving my job, the world slowed down with the arrival of the pandemic. That first year filled with stillness, isolation, and deep personal loss, was heavier on my heart than any before it. The lessons were hard, but some were as gentle as the winter sun. Obhigata was born from the loss of my father during the pandemic: a grief I wish on no one. What followed was a quiet, growing closeness with my mother, and from this, Magic & Mothers emerged, a reminder of the invisible threads that hold us together. Money and Me, Un-Marriage-Able, and Consent were hard earned lessons, shaped by age, independence, and the slow drawing of personal boundaries. An Ode to the Cat That Went Away is my love letter to Chengiz, my first adopted cat, who I co-parented with my then partner, his name-giver. I often feel that as the love between two people faded, so did Chengiz, marking the quiet death of all that was false and performative. Each of these moments offered me the strength to bloom, in time, into the person I was meant to become.

And then came the Spring collection. Quietly, and then all at once. A dog and his man entered my life, two souls whose quiet companionship taught me the true meaning of relationships. Their gentle, nurturing bond stole my heart a hundred times over. Comparison was a hard lesson to swallow, one that often visits anyone starting from scratch. Understanding it taught me patience and compassion, two things I now hold close. After all, everyone needs a soft hug beside every hard lesson. An Entrepreneur's Dream is the ongoing journey of trying to build something on my own, while dreaming relentlessly. Asking for Help is a reminder to myself that bravery often begins with vulnerability. Spring is a season of hard work, and perhaps the hardest work is figuring out who we truly are, especially when life challenges us the most. Whatever effort we put in here is our way of offering something back to the world — the simplest way to say thank you for the life we've been given.

The Summer collection is both a personal joy to read and to have lived. Every poem in this section is laced with hope. Hope for myself, for my life, for all of us, and for the quiet victory of the individual spirit within the greater whole. My Sister and I, is an ode to the one who walks this earth beside me — always has, always will. We were never "friends," but always something more, something kept on a pedestal. Over time, I believe the poem will unfold into truth as life unfolds for us both. Friendship Fades is my personal anthem, a song I lived long before I wrote it. For me, friendships, like seasons, shift and change, but they leave us with new ones along the way, over and over. I dream of a life where I carry everyone I meet along with me; that is the kind of dream I dream most often. An Adoption Dilemma is a playful, satirical piece about my resistance to adopt my dog Phoebe, who, without me realising, had long since adopted me. It is the kind of push-and-pull I usually associate with romance, but in truth, Phoebe might just be my soulmate. Building a Home is an ongoing, surreal act for me, one I tend to, quietly, day after day. If you know just one thing about me, know this: I am always building, always moving toward that home. Wintering Gracefully is my hope for all of us. May we age not only with grace but with kindness for all that we will someday leave behind. As a writer, I do not wish for apocalyptic endings, only fairy tales — the kind with mermaids and queens.

And so, this collection rests in your hands.
Every poem is a piece of a life lived with curiosity, love,

and the quiet courage to begin again. I hope these words
meet you gently, like an old friend or a long-forgotten
memory. I hope they remind you — as they reminded me
— that life is rarely linear, but always rich with lessons,
and that the world around us, in its oddness and beauty,
is always nurturing.
Thank you for reading and for letting these words sit
beside you, even if only for a little while.

Acknowledgements

To all my friends,
you have introduced me to Love.
Thank You.

To my Sister, Jiju and Bianca,
Thank you for being my Strength and backbone.

To Haruki Murakami,
Thank you for introducing me to Magic.

To this world and everything in it
Thank you for being a muse

To Sadness and Loss,

Thank you for offering the greatest lessons

To Love,

You will be my end and my beginning.
and I will be your believer forever.

Non-Linear Living

Does an ant follow a *linear* path?
I wondered.
So I went looking for an ant.

In the deep creases of the city,
I found a few,
lurking in temporary holes.

One sighed, looking at me
as if she already knew
exactly why I was there.

"No linear paths here, madam.
We chase only
what nourishes us back.
But that's the kind of question
you never ask."

But you live in groups,
March in your mother's troops.
How would you then, Madam Ant,
know where I am at?

She sighed again,
heavier this time,
frail beside her hill,
her body, a testament of will.

Then, almost gently,
she offered a simple truth;

*"Humans know how to destroy
and then call it design.*

*It's only in your better health
you begin to desire.
Desire more.*

*Carve your own path.
See if your mother follows.*

*Whether it is sweet
or a grain of salt.
what you find
will only be yours.*

*And still, you'll ask
Does an ant follow a path?*

No, they make their own
Yet they do it together".

Quitting Your Job

How is it, that from the day you step in,
to a fluorescent-lit office,
you dream of quitting your job?

To do what?
Shepherd goats in the misty mountains,
where the cold wind hums of freedom,
and the blue sky stretches wide?

Why is it,
that from the moment your manager screams,
you dream of quitting your job?
To sip sangria with friends at sunset,
Their laughter, your biggest attachment.

Be honest,
when you first memorise the brand mission,
Don't you dream of quitting your job?
To stand at afternoon arrivals,
arms open for family,
or stir a leisurely-cooked meal
that tastes of home.

For God's sake,

from the day you get your first paycheck,
And your quiet bondage begins
you do dream of quitting your job!
To be your own boss, write books, buy plants,
Retire, growing coriander, doing a little dance.

I wish, then
from the day you sign, the black and white fate,
you dream not just of quitting,
But of building a life
that does not fit inside a resume.

So go, my friend,
lover of freedom, seeker of a simpler life.
Go quit that job of your latent dreams.
Take an afternoon nap, dream freely
Start round two, there is no refund.
Life is but an endless wave,
For you to ride with wild abandon.

Pancake & Love

I made my first pancake when I turned twenty-nine,
Perhaps the pressure of a decade turning in.
Mom made them, my friends did too,
And finally, it was time for me to start whippin'.

Pancakes, in all their shapes and tastes,
Had my fancy since childhood.
Mom served them hot,
like *DDLJ* serving romance.

Oh, the delight!
Honey dripping, fuelling a sugar rush,
Romancing my body.
The aroma teased me,
Like warm kisses held back on a rainy day.
Love and pancakes intertwined in innocent times.
A shapely bowl was easier to find,

So I gathered my fears and ingredients together.
But nothing prepared me for the tsunami of gooeyness.
Burning on the stove, hot and low.
Mushy, icky, uncooked mess,
Sweeping over the pan like a virus.
Batter spilled on my clothes, mocking me,

Like my messy life spilling over the decade's coffin.

That's when the heat spoke.
Agreed, you won't believe me.
Let your hands burn, once or twenty times.
Let your heart grieve the mushy slime.

Flour is a delicate product of patience,
and whip that egg with all the kindness you got.
Food is a living being, much like a lover,
To be coaxed and cuddled with sugar and salt.

Fearless we must be in cooking and love,
For what we give is what we reap.
And just like that, it all came together.
Why quitting is never the answer to desire.

So I lick the batter off, like a wounded tiger.
And pick up the ladle,
To begin a new love affair.

Of Pens And Dreams- A Writer's Dilemma

Unpublished crafts,
half-written drafts,
a muse that both torments and inspires.

Clutching at paper, flying away.
Oh, bizarre god of words,
Weaver of tangled thoughts.

Do you bless or burden me?
 Would you delay this deadline?
Would you soften the brief,
Make it kind?

Spirits of authors I have read
float nearby, screaming high,
"Rephrase! Restructure! Change!"
"Adapt, compare, but be original!"
Fact check, connect, praise.
Carve, erase, carve again,
Until only the bones remain.
Once a dream, now it's dead.

Yet I dream, of a child far away,

Quoting me, smiling during day,
Lazing in bed, devouring each page,
breathing heavy as it ends.

Write, you fool. Get your head straight.
Spill your silences into ink
Live more. Think less.
Don't hide,
Show yourself.

Your true self, draped in fantasy.
No one guesses. No one believes.
Could it be true?
My life, yours to see,
to reject, relive, reassess.

And so, I place this stone
in surrender, an offering
a weight at my heart's centre,
where all words begin.

Therapy & I

I broke up with my therapist,
and this is my second innings.
The end of healing can feel like a heartbreak,
yet hold the quiet thrill of beginnings.

I first sought help at twenty-one,
filling forms in sterile halls,
wandering through white cubicles
losing my way more than once.

The right fit never came at the right time,
It was 2011, and they were not kind.
Still, I kept going, fighting with life,
each step inching toward feeling aligned.

Then I met her, my refuge,
home for my shadows to finally rest.
I didn't need a lover after all,
but someone who deeply listened instead.

Therapy and I grew together,
side by side, hands intertwined.
Tears gently wiped away,
intricately de-tangling my messy mind.

Through betrayals, guilt, and choked-up throat
I clung to life like a single, fragile rope.
They called her a therapist,
to me, she was my life giving trope.

You can imagine why a breakup was never planned.
But it was she who had transformed me,
made me fuller.

Some goodbyes are bitter to swallow,
but my healed heart finally learned
to let go.

Threshold Of A Mid-Life Crisis

They say at 29, you lose sight of your life,
or look too closely at this cold world, trying to thrive.
A mystery unfolds, and your heart quietly tries
To understand what it means to be alive.

Meditate. Close your eyes,
but only if you ask the questions right.
Answers will come, clarity might prevail.
Inhale, exhale, and drop that weight.

The forest heals, nature pulls you in,
asking gently to reveal the truth within.
Therapy is abundant, yoga brings you home,
and talking to your friends never gets old.

Maybe travel is the only plan.
Pack your bags and walk Buddha's path.
Abandon the known, delete the apps,
Let quiet reflection balance chaos and calm.

You enter your 30s with battlefields in mind,
Earning the space to reflect and shine.
Choosing a partner or a retirement plan

None of it is linear, none of it kind.

Because life in your 30s is meant to be tested.
You're wiser, braver, for all that's manifested.
Life isn't happening *to* you, it's happening *for* you.
A warrior and a wanderer, still fighting, still learning.

An Ode To The Cat That Went Away

Chengiz purred the night he found
his brother's body, still and round,
out in the road where streetlights stretch,
crushed beneath an iron hound.

They grew up twinned, two paws in a step,
but now the world had lost its depth.
Nothing he did could bring him back
So Chengiz tried to stay on track.

He braved the snow, the barking wet dogs.
His mother nuzzled him, soft but lost.
Through winter's hush he curled to sleep,
Dreaming of climbing those apple trees
Teasing dogs and hunting pigeons
Rubbing his hips in grassy ribbons.

Chengiz roamed untamed and tall,
Leaping windows, scaling walls
The night, the sky, the earth- his own
A kingdom full of secret stones.

He brought back trophies, rats and snakes,

laid them down for his mother's sake,
silent gifts from wild trade,
tokens of a life tamed, yet untamed.

Then one day, a tiny thing came
soft and strange, a purring blame.
She stole his place in his mother's arms,
Chengiz was kind, but not one to share.

So when the moon hung, long and low,
Chengiz slipped into orchard's shadow,
Will-fully he chose his destiny,
Unapologetically building, a wild legacy

Obigata- The honour of grief

When my father's lungs were eaten away,
slowly, by a virus they called COVID,
it left me a gift I never asked for,
while taking my best man away.

"Obhigata," they call it in my native tongue
a word that rolls off the lips like a gentle breeze,
yet hides in its depths the sharpest crevices,
carrying bitter truths that changes you forever.

A simple word for *gathering experience,*
always spoken to offer strength.
a way to find meaning in failure,
a balm for aching hearts to vent.

"Oh, you lost so-and-so, but you gained obhigata,"
They say,
as if wisdom were a fair exchange for love.
As if falling too hard grants you certification
an honorary title in grief's hall of fame.

Now, I face a harsher world alone,
but I carry this currency, this certificate of sorrow.

I am richer for the tears I've collected,
yet quiet strength is my only reward
And grief is meant to be a sword.

You see, the certificate is not truly mine
they can take it away anytime.
For calmness is *adulthood,*
And anger is for those who only whine.

But I would trade this wisdom in an instant.
tear it up, set it ablaze
for my father's laughter in the golden afternoons,
for the stories he told, the lessons he left unspoken.

I wanted to grow old
with him watching my journey,
to see his smile on his 80th birthday,
to gift him my success, my stories, my time
to show him how much *obhigata* I had gained,
with him still standing beside me.

Instead, I hold nothing but experience
of grief, of joy, of the silences in between.
A collection of memories, questions with no answers,
and the weight of becoming an adult,
in the sorrow of missing him every day.

Money & Me

I used to dream of living off-grid,
never needing money,
never giving a damn.

A fantasy we all share,
even with full bank accounts,
life feels like a scam.

I thought I didn't need money,
until a hospital bill said *no insurance claim.*
A broken tooth, a plane ticket,
 whispering my name again.

When money runs low,
so does my peace.
visions of sidewalks,
replacing Excel sheets.

The fear of being forgotten,
unseen, not enough,
of never tasting the luxuries
I once dreamt of.

But when I have too much,

it's just paper and dust.
No thrill, no joy, no sense of a win
just dry days and drier thoughts.

I close my eyes and picture a field,
a cabin, a mountain, a place to be still.
Running away with my friends and my love,
somewhere quiet, just time to kill.

But even there,
money will knock.
Too little, too much,
they call it luck.
We won't take it with us when we go,
but while we're here,
make life richer than gold.

Magic and Mothers

Don't you think they are magical beings?
Everything they touch supernaturally heals.
The crumpled shirt, the water warmed,
The silent presence of things rearranged.

I carry the weight of the world,
Bruised lips, secrets hidden even from myself.
She hands me a glass of water,
presses fingers into my hair,
and I dissolve like sugar in tea.

They tell me,
"Thirty-five and single?
It's time to build a home."
I glance at her, my only dome.

At the railway station, I clasp her hand.
Softness from me, she never demands.
Yet in the next breath,
I rest against her shoulder,
kiss the soft map of arms that are older,

Just like that,

roles reversed,
by time's changing winds.

She is ageing,
and I cannot even write the words.
My chest tightens, my eyes burn.

I wish time would forget her name,
let the years pass without a trace.
Yet she drifts like autumn leaves,
Swaying and glowing, lullaby dreams.

Perhaps angels exist after all,
because I have known mine all along.

Consent

I reserve my consent,
in the form of dissent.
You can have your opinions
Just don't shove them in my face.

You are allowed your fears.
But you and I
are not the same tier.

I am a person
of vivid mistakes,
unkempt dreams,
and petty heartaches.

I don't like it linear,
neat, or tidy.
My life is a worn-out chessboard,
muddy shoes,
recycled clothes.
They call me Heidi.

Consent is my fortress.
Attention, my temple.
Maybe I am a victim.

An unpopular hermit.
But most goons I see around
think of giving me a permit.

Lies and quick content.
Enough to keep them content.
Still,
I will guard the door to my attention.
It is not yours to bend.

I refuse to lie lonely,
shivering in a shed,
praising and pleading
to all that is said.
I am wilful.
Nasty.
A witch, of sorts.
I choose to withhold
what comes at personal cost.

So yes,
I do reserve my consent,
in the form of
 dirty dissent.

12. Un-Marriage-able

A match made in heaven!
That's how it was sold before.
Now, marriage is complicated
harder to believe it will endure.

We walk in with egos,
identities, and carefully guarded wounds.
We celebrate what makes us strange.
Then wonder why no one fits like a glove.

Are you open-minded?
Willing to bruise in a healthy fight?
Can you love through a mess
that won't be cleaned overnight?

Equal partnership
may still be a hopeful dream.
Some get lemon,
and some get melon.
Life levels us eventually,
but never all at once.

Pain doesn't check schedules.
Grief won't sync its clock.

Maybe that's where we break,
tired of waiting for their storm to break?

Am I winning
if I collapse into the star shining brightly?
Or if I quietly
hold the line
on who we are, selfishly?

You become a family
until someone says,
Stop calling me that.
And just like that,
the way gets lost.
No compass, no maps,
just a restart.

So I share my fear,
trying to be a dreamer,
craving the title of *Mrs*
hiding demons in their lair.

Titles won't save us.
Whether alone or together.
We still have to become
our own person, forever.

Comparison - The Chronic Ache

What is the comparison,
between the sun and the moon?
Stars and rainbows?
Mountains and meadows?

One shade of blue cannot be compared
to another.
Like a painted dawn
or a friend's goodbye.

Neither can the loss of love
be weighed against
the loss of respect.
Can it?

Still, we wake each morning,
ignoring the imprints of our DNA
to scroll through numbers,
to check a bank balance
against someone else's worth.

We feel the sting of jealousy
like salt pressed against skin,

and wear the weight of guilt
Distinguished as a crown.

Am I better for wanting more?
Unsure if I want it,
or is it that I want
her spotlight instead?

I don't feel the wanting
Only the absence.
Losing grip,
spiralling down.
I live in my head,
leaving no space,
for reality.

Seeing the pattern
doesn't save us.
We stay buckled in,
In this highway to hell,
we hardly know
how to pull the lever.

To stop!
This world is on a shiny display.
And we are sanding ourselves smooth,

to fit the clean cubicles and tailored resumes.
Erasing our edges, spoiling our youth.

A Dog And His Man

She is sure he is dreaming some days,
lying on the couch, eyes lost in the glow of the TV,
blaring noise, a distant echo to his wandering mind.
The man she loves, lays still,
unaware of his own serendipity.

Her tongue out in the sun,
Her golden glow of pride.
Her restless energy,
always makes him smile.

He takes her along on his silent adventures,
Rolling down hills, chasing spring together.
Then friends come along, wild and loyal as him.
She is happier, when they have more to share.

His friends help him,
look after her all day long.
Curled on the couch,
his hand on her belly,
she hopes they love him as she does.

And she? She dreams of a shire,
Endless golden fields to her heart's desire.

toys thrown, tugged, and chased till the stars fade.
Licking, playing, loving—until eternity rolls away.

An Entrepreneur's Poem

I meant to tell a gentle story,
but became, instead, an entrepreneur.
Trading calm for chaos,
hoping one day I'd grow mature.

Doing it alone, holding storms at bay,
I dive into panic and clarity alike.
Just to land a little farther each day,
Five W's and one H dance through my psyche.

Everything's tagged, *made with love*.
But where does my rising anger rest?
I race myself, count fragile chances,
As frustration builds inside my chest.
Doubts creep quietly,
splitting me in half,
What if I'm not that tough?
Never enough?

How do I sell without hurting myself?
The sheets don't balance.
My heart stays rough.

Faltering a thousand times, I rise,

new skills honed,
patience now my armour.

Every endless road needs grit and grace,
Breathing life into dreams,
will be the summit's honour.

Asking For Help

Do I seem like the type to ask for help?
Oh no—I'm the tough kind,
with an ironclad heart
that keeps me sane.

I wear my mask better than most,
hiding bad days beneath steady gaze.
You cry in cubicles,
but I dry your tears,
offering reason when emotions flare.

Logic and hard work always win the race,
at least, that's what my father would say.

You may not know me,
but know this well,
I am a priest of fear,
A conqueror on sale.

I have faith in being the pillar,
With nowhere left to run,
Never asking for help.
Because I am a superhero to someone.

I shatter in empty cars,
scream where no one listens,
but you will never see me cry,
without your permission.

Lovers call me closed-off,
A shipwreck at the dock.
My parents could only afford,
Deep silence and a frock.

Asking for help is overrated.
That's where our weakness lies
Yet, when I offer it to others,
I see light return to their eyes.

And I wonder,
was I wrong?
to stop believing in
a hopeful song?

An Adoption Dilemma

It's strange, when you think,
Phoebe didn't choose me,
yet she did.
I thought I chose her,
yet somehow, I didn't.

With big black eyes,
she captured every scene
A mother, a guardian,
a self-proclaimed queen.
Yet, when I was alone,
she sought me out,
as if to say,
the crown was mine.

At first, she came wagging twice a day,
stealing a bite from every plate.
Come winter morning, she brought her pups,
frustrated in her vulnerable state.

Five at first, then three,
then came the fever,
It left just one.
Phoebe stayed strong,

raising Jacob alone,
but come fall, he too,
leaves her and move on.

And then there were two
Phoebe and I,
an adopted house,
and maybe an adopted dog.
But in truth, I did have a choice,
to treat her better,
to give her a voice.

She had been left before.
As seen in her restless eyes,
searching each night
a place to rest her sight,
But bracing,
for yet another *no*.

So how can I claim this choice is mine,
when people look at her and say she is *mine?*
Our wild abandon,
love and longing song,
she has already chosen me,
given me a place to belong.

Building A Home

I never thought I'd build myself a home
In my twenties, renting was easy.
Real estate - never a dream.
But maybe it wasn't the houses I hated,
just the lifeless concrete boxes,
stacked up to steal the sky.

Childhood was spent on open terraces,
dangling from window sills,
fingers grazing mango leaves.

Eating kulfis, crappy bhel,
watching monkeys swing away,
Where no noise, only laughter lived.

So I left the city, silently one night,
frustrated by a foggy future,
a faltering love life.

Only to arrive in a village bathed in sun,
where the air smelled of ripe fruit,
where childhood felt close again.

I lingered there, in its peachy warmth,

watching a tiny house perched on a cliff.

For years, I only admired it,
until I realised.
I was longing, truly longing,
for a home of my own.

For the love of my own quiet space,
craving cosy, lazy, mindless days.
And visits from loved ones
who might eventually stay,

But longing is easy.
Bricks and beams, a harder dream.
And then a silent fear crept in.

Fear of growing up too fast,
or maybe of growing alone at last?

A house needs hands to build it,
but what of arms to hold me?

Sharing a sofa,
arguing over curtains and cupboard space,
filling kitchen shelves with someone else's taste.

Was I afraid of the silence?

or of being left to stray?

But then, I gave my life a hard glance.
I had been alone all along.
Holding myself up so long,
Perhaps, I had done well after all.

So I decided,
love can wait,
but the home cannot.

And so, I stepped to the cliff's edge,
the wind rushing past,
whispering my name.
And at last,
I came alive.

Will I die here alone?
I'll never know.
But I can wait for life's mystery to unfold,
and still have a home of my own.

Sister's Paradox

We are good for each other,
Funny, smart, a little insane.
Born from a family of do-gooders,
Finding eventually, our own lane.

She is seven years ahead of me,
Wiser, fitter, never a quitter.
The insurance to my injuries,
My protector and my babysitter.

Through winding roads of life we tread,
She leads the way, I follow near.
Lessons learned by walking behind her,
Her wisdom echoes, loud and clear.

She fears at times.
But that's just life.
She screams for space,
Yet hugs too tight.

We mirror souls, yet differ still,
A quiet storm, a golden light.
Her logic reigns, while I embrace
The restless pull of endless night.

I idolised her from the start,
But now, in my own steady prime,
I need her not just as my guide,
But as my warmth through fleeting time.

We've grown and changed, yet stayed aligned.
She raised a child, yet raised me too.
Through trials and endless waves we ride.
We learned to finally say, I love you.

One day, as silver streaks our hair,
We'll share stories, we'll sing old songs,
I'll braid her hair, she'll bake for me,
And time will flow like gentle streams.

Friendship Fades

They told us friendship fades, didn't they?
When we lied just to play in the streets a little longer.
They told us, didn't they?
'Friends don't last! focus on your exams'.

When we skipped class, laughing in the rain,
They shook their heads. *'It wont last'* they'd say
'Friendship expires, so you better prepare
For a lonely life filled with books and forms to fill'.

When cities changed, and we tried to stay in touch,
They warned, *'time changes everything,*
So don't get your hopes up too high
Friendships are GPS-based'.

When friends picked you up from broken bars
After a night of disastrous first date,
You heard their whispers but ignored them,
The voice saying, *'this will all fade'.*

When friends came to your wedding and danced till
dawn,
The sceptics smirked, *'what's the big deal?*
Friendships are for sharing joy,

but in sorrow, You will stand alone'.

When friends were the first to know,
you had cheated on your dame,
They didn't judge. They gave you courage,
To face yourself in the mirror again.

But the voices never stopped,
Echoing the same old warnings, again and again,
'Friendship will falter, in misfortune,
Leave you alone, take you for granted'.

And yet, with decades behind me,
I stand beside friends who never left.
Their voices slowly faded out.
My faith restored, friends can last a lifetime.

Wintering Gracefully

I feel old,
not too old, though.
Wisdom arrives late,
when I am out of breath.

Funny, this world.
Lessons come through bruises.
Nothing they can steal from you
can be rebuilt with obedience.

Leaving my 20s,
confident and proud,
ego in my pocket,
echoing verses loud.

Leaving my 30s,
the climb grows steeper.
Silver strands, I welcome,
but my thoughts stretch thinner.

I stand like a mountain now,
weathered, but upright.
I flow like a river,
softened, but,

open to uprise.

I drift like a cloud,
detached yet strong,
watching youth pass me
like my favorite childhood song.

Aging isn't like wine.
It doesn't always refine.
Sometimes, it just aches.
And calls for a stronger spine.

Now a leader, also a wanderer,
yet my compass often wavers.
I think of aches and bank accounts,
half-spoken dreams
of a quieter haven.

I advise, I dictate,
ask others to be kind.
But beneath that,
I crave kindness
from time's side.

I've traded moments
for memories.
And still,

I hide
more than I reveal.

All I ask now
is not youth again
just graceful wintering.
No loss, no gain.

www.ingramcontent.com/pod-product-compliance
Lightning Source LLC
LaVergne TN
LVHW050936200726
843508LV00011B/2354